EVOLVE your HABITS

Zoe McKey is a Communication and Lifestyle Coach based in Los Angeles, California.

She studied in international and social studies for her bachelor's and master's degrees. Being an avid student of human behaviour, psychology, and healthy connections, she has spent more than 400 hours in therapy, journaled 1000+ pages, and read over 300 books on the topics of communication, self-discovery, and self-improvement.

For 10 years, she's been helping people discover how to live the life they want. Zoe has a profound understanding on what it takes to gain self-understanding, get unstuck, and reach new levels of growth and fulfilment. She has written over 30 books on these subjects that have been translated in multiple languages around the globe.

EVOLVE your HABITS
Become Who You Want to Be

ZOE MCKEY

Published by
Rupa Publications India Pvt. Ltd 2024
7/16, Ansari Road, Daryaganj
New Delhi 110002

Sales centres:
Bengaluru Chennai
Hyderabad Jaipur Kathmandu
Kolkata Mumbai Prayagraj

Copyright © Zoe McKey 2024
Published under arrangement with
Zoe McKey through TLL Literary Agency

The views and opinions expressed in this book are the author's own and the facts are as reported by her which have been verified to the extent possible, and the publishers are not in any way liable for the same.

All rights reserved.
No part of this publication may be reproduced, transmitted, or stored in a retrieval system, in any form or by any means, electronic, mechanical, photocopying, recording or otherwise, without the prior permission of the publisher.

P-ISBN: 978-93-5702-662-8
E-ISBN: 978-93-5702-819-6

First impression 2024

10 9 8 7 6 5 4 3 2 1

The moral right of the author has been asserted.

Printed in India

This book is sold subject to the condition that it shall not, by way of trade or otherwise, be lent, resold, hired out, or otherwise circulated, without the publisher's prior consent, in any form of binding or cover other than that in which it is published.

Contents

1. The Truth about Changing — 1
2. What Is Human Behavior? — 8
3. What Is Behavioral Change? — 18
4. The Transtheoretical Model — 27
5. Why Do You Resist Change? — 36
6. Why'd You Buy This Book? — 45
7. How Do You Start Changing? — 53
8. How Do You Eat an Elephant? — 60
9. Two Key Activities for Lasting Change — 65
10. New Habits for a New Life — 75

Conclusion — 82
References — 85
Endnotes — 88

1
The Truth about Changing

Change is never easy, but it is necessary sometimes. I remember how crazy everyone thought I was when I decided to drop out of university, quit my job, travel, and work from my computer as a writer. It does sound pretty crazy when you lay it all out there. Everyone said that I was giving up the security of a normal life where I could go to school and get a desk job.

I'll admit, changing everything in my life so drastically led to a lot of hardship, especially in the beginning. However, it did lead to some really blissful decisions and let me learn a great deal in my twenties so I inflicted the least possible damage on my life. My motto is to fail early, if you're going to do it. Fail early, and fail big time. Fail gloriously, miserably, heartbreakingly, and in the end—educationally. There's nothing wrong with failure!

This being said, you shouldn't chase failure, or think that tons of failures are normal. If you can help it, don't fail. Do your best and aim for success. But if you must fail and learn some lessons in life (which everybody must), it is better to do it earlier than later.

When you're young, your talent isn't the best thing about you. Neither are your ideas or your experience. People probably spend all day telling you how important talent and experience is, but I'm here to tell you that your greatest asset is actually your time. You have a lot more time than someone in their forties or fifties, and that allows you to make mistakes and take bigger risks. It's still scary, but you're much better off now to drop everything and travel or start up the blog that you've been dreaming of.

When you're younger, you don't often have the financial responsibilities of an older adult. There's usually not a family to provide for, and while the prospect of getting some work experience and paying off the mountain of debt is surely tempting, a few years doesn't make a difference. There is virtually no difference between a 21-year-old and a 25-year-old with a mountain of debt and zero work experience.

Being young comes with advantages. Sure, you might not be as experienced as you will be later in life, but that's what's so great about it. You can fail, and you can learn from those failures so that later on, and evolve better habits eventually. There are a lot of reasons people refuse to make changes, but these excuses are just that—excuses!

Most of the time, we think that youth goes with advances. You think of the Nobel Prize winners, people like Einstein, and suddenly you're feeling pretty useless. The great thing is that these people are actually much older than you think. Their innovations came at a later age (50, on average), so age being an excuse for not changing is not acceptable.

If you ask a kid to jump on the monkey bars and try them out, they're going to immediately go. Even if they fail, which they probably will, they still get up and try it, if you ask them to. However, ask an adult to go on the monkey bars and they'll start to panic. "Oh, no, I don't have the upper body strength. I don't even know how to do monkey bars!"

If we were just a little more like kids, we might actually enjoy change and learn something amazing. Instead, we get stuck in our comfort zones. Our curiosity is gone. We all know the saying, "Curiosity killed the cat." However, that's said by adults who don't want to share something and who are far past their age of curiosity. We really like our comfort zones, and they're called comfort zones for a reason.

More than two years ago, I decided to quit my job. I quit the university as well and left Hungary for good. In truth, I went to travel to follow someone that I love, and luckily all turned out well. Despite the challenges that came along with some people not agreeing with my choice, I decided to do it anyway. Sure, I got cut away from the people I knew, and that wasn't really fun, but everything else was amazing.

If I'd never made that decision to become a writer and travel, I wouldn't have become the person I am today. Now I've traveled to almost 50 countries, I've met exceptional people, and I've even learned a new language! It's been an amazing experience, but I'm still challenging myself. I'm expanding my online work, I'm writing books, and I've embraced a minimalistic lifestyle.

I'm not saying that you need to drop everything and move to another country, but I am saying that you need to challenge yourself. Nothing good comes from our comfort zones. It's when we reach outside our comfort that we can really have amazing experiences.

Also, amazing possibilities are born in the ashes of failures. When I broke up with my previous boyfriend, I was alone, juggling with two jobs, heartbroken, and the only thing I could do to escape was to hitchhike to Italy for two weeks (consuming all my holiday period at work)… It is warmer to sleep on the streets over there, I thought. Thankfully, I didn't have to sleep on the streets—some amazing people I met during my hitchhike were in desperate need of a babysitter for their cats for one and a half week or so. During this period I met the love of my life. That's how my writing and traveling journey started…

Everything was so unexpected. One moment I felt like I was living in pure bliss, finding love in a magical place. And the next, I was thrown upside-down and confused on what I was going to do with life to be able to follow him to the United States. I made the crazy, unexpected decision to give up everything, publish my first book and pursue happiness in a new way. Was it risky? Sure thing. Was it uncomfortable? Oh, boy... Insecurity felt like hell!

Unexpected events are always affecting our lives. Of course, I thought about going back sometimes to my old life, I had moths of procrastination, of disbelief, of mental nihilism during my first year as a writer. I wanted to give up so many times... But luckily, it did work out as time passed. I learned an important lesson during my years of renaissance.

Whenever we are faced with something unexpected, we freak out. We resist changing at all, and it actually causes us more suffering in the long run. Our mindsets and behaviors need to be prepared for the unexpected. Just like you stretch before an intense workout, we need to stretch out our minds to prepare. I know it sounds impossible to prepare for the unexpected, but really we are just helping ourselves so that when the unexpected does happen, we aren't going to completely collapse. If we try to prepare ourselves mentally to face dramatic events, this practice eventually creates a habit change in our behavior. We'll become conditioned to handle the unexpected changes with a much calmer and collected attitude.

Let's be honest: change can really hurt sometimes. It can tear our hearts apart, it can kick us down, and when it rains, it always pours. But grab your umbrella, because it hurts a hell of a lot less if you are prepared to deal with change. I'm going to help you out with that in this book.

Evolve Your Habits

Change can be a threat to us, which activates our fight-or-flight response. It's a stress stimulus that happens in unexpected or dangerous situations. The interesting thing is that our relationship with change is a paradox.

Although we admire people who make changes, we have a very hard time changing ourselves. We know that change is required in life, and yet we don't prepare for our own change. Unfortunately, change is really important. While it would be nice for everything to stay the same, change is actually the only thing you can rely on in life.

I mean, seriously, think about it. Every day you think that nothing is changing, but it really is. You get up in the morning older than you were the day before, you make a subtle change in your daily routine, and things change. Friendships end, relationships end, businesses fail, and people get fired. At the same time, friendships get stronger, relationships evolve to the next level, someone makes her first million, and someone finds a job. Everything is changing constantly!

In your personal and professional life, being able to adapt to a situation is a competitive advantage. When life throws you sour lemons, you have to try and still make lemonade. Just like Darwin concluded, "Not the strongest or the smartest survives on the long run, but the one most adaptive to changes." The people who look at the sour lemons and say, "There's no way lemonade can be made from this. Sorry," are the people who are not going to adapt to change. Now imagine if you were the person who said, "Yeah, I can work with this! Even though I was expecting some sweet apples, I'll make do." Who do you think people are going to want to be around?

I know it's not an overnight process in learning to adapt to change, but I'm prepared to help you rethink change in creative terms that can make you passionate and enduring.

My book is about to teach you how to create change in your behavior and adopt good habits to sustain these changes. Not only that, but you're going to learn how to embrace it. And don't worry; I've used some scientifically proven techniques so that you will be doing things that are proven to help you. So buckle up, it's going to be one amazing journey!

Key Takeaways:

- Change isn't easy, but it is necessary.
- Don't be afraid to take chances, especially when you are young.
- Be more curious, become like a child again!
- Comfort zones only hurt you in the end.
- You can prepare your mind to change.
- Adaptability will become a great advantage.

2

What Is Human Behavior?

Human behavior—you're probably shaking your head and saying, "Uh, duh, of course I know what that is." I mean, it's what we do on a daily basis! It is our ultimate habit arsenal–our behavior. We behave. Well, most of the time, right?

All jokes aside, do we really know what human behavior is? Sure, we live it every day. But owning an apron doesn't make you a chef. We need to understand what's needed to change human behavior; otherwise we'll never succeed in changing our own behavior.

First, we have to identify what it is that we want to change. Maybe we want to change a bad habit we have, maybe we want to switch jobs, or maybe we just want to change our life for the better. Either way, learning about human behavior helps us understand what needs to be done to make a permanent and lasting change.

The scientific definition of human behavior is that

it's the responses we make in response to external or internal stimuli. It's our physical actions and our observable emotions that happen within us. Your temperament or personality is probably pretty consistent, but as we grow older, our behaviors change. When someone takes away a toy from a child, they get frustrated, scream, and throw a tantrum. However, when that child grows older, it's not as big of a deal if someone wants to play with one of their toys or borrow their belongings. Human behavior is dictated by age, genetics, and driven by thoughts and feelings. However, ethics, authority, coercion, and even persuasion can affect our behavior.

Behavior is either acceptable, strange, or unacceptable. See, it's totally okay for someone to wake up and grab a cup of coffee. It might be a bit strange for someone to add butter to his or her coffee, but it's acceptable. What is not acceptable is taking a hot cup of coffee and throwing it at someone. Most of these behaviors have pretty self-explanatory criteria when it comes to whether they are acceptable or not. Each person produces different behaviors in response to different stimuli, and social norms often affect our behavior.

There are five factors that create our behavioral responses. These are genetics, social norms, creativity, core faith and culture, and attitude.[1]

We've known for quite some time that genetics can influence how a person behaves. There's an argument about nature versus nurture, basically meaning how much of our genetics make up our behavior? And how much of our nurture (or lack of it) makes up our behavior? Genetics play some part in how a person behaves. For example, addiction or depression may run in the family, and that could impact how resilient a person is when faced with a stimulus like alcohol or grief.

This is not exclusive to humans, and there have been a lot of studies with animals and the genetics from their parents as well. Just because your father was an alcoholic doesn't mean that you will be, but it does mean that you are predisposed to addiction if you find yourself in that situation. And if your mother was extremely spontaneous and you're as introverted as they come, that doesn't mean that you were picked up from the side of the road. Some people are going to act a lot like their parents while others won't. However, we do know that our behavior is somewhat influenced by the genes our biological parents have given us.[2]

The second factor, social norms, is what everyone else does in a society that is deemed normal. This shapes both our behaviors and attitudes. Sometimes social norms have a negative connotation. I mean, who wants to blend in with the crowd? What's interesting is that social norms are actually what cause our society to function like it does. Because it affects most people who are in a group, their behavior is more likely to be in line with social norms.

Now, this can be a good and a bad thing. For example, we all know it's bad to steal things. Because the social

What Is Human Behavior?

norm is that it's not okay to steal something, most people aren't going to be stealing anytime soon. Of course, there are some outliers who will still steal, but the majority of us don't. It can also be positive, like everyone dressing warmer in the winter. Wearing a tank top in the snow is generally considered strange, and most people are going to dress warmly because everyone else is dressing warmly.

Social norms rely on the desire to be accepted by everyone else around you. We all want to fit in, and so social norms work. Without them, we'd have to make a lot more choices and our behaviors would become more abstract.[3]

The third factor is creativity. You may think that you're either creative or you're not, but everyone has some level of creativity inside them. This is a very important factor, because it is creativity that helps you to break outside of your comfort zone. I'm sure you can think of someone in your life who's awesomely creative, but creativity is something we all use in our daily routines, like when you find a shortcut to your work when traffic is heavy, or even if you find a way to stuff a bunch of food into a container that should definitely not hold that much food (we've all been there). These little things make us creative, and because of that, they are part of our human behavior.

The fourth factor is core faith and culture. A lot of us confuse faith with religion, and that's not necessarily true. Faith can be shown in religion, but it can also be shown in philosophy, or your cultural and personal beliefs.

When we have faith in something, it affects how we act. Maybe we have faith in karma, so we don't get mad when something bad happens because whatever goes around comes around. Or maybe we have faith in a higher power that is looking out for us, so we treat a breakup as just another door being closed.[4]

In the United States alone, 80% of people claim to have a belief in some sort of higher power, which definitely affects human behavior. What goes hand in hand with faith is your morals. Obviously, believing in a religion teaches you that you shouldn't steal. However, you might also hold this moral because you believe in karma or something else.

Regardless of what you believe in, you have a set of morals. Maybe your set of morals is something like never eating food past the expiration date and always making sure to turn the lights off when you leave. Or maybe your morals are to treat everyone kindly and do no harm. But to make things easy, let's say you hold the moral of always turning the light off when you leave. And then let's say you forgot to turn the light off when you left this morning.[5] *Gasp!*

What are you feeling right now? You're probably feeling uncomfortable and guilty. Your mind is chastising you. "Darn it, Susan, why'd you forget to turn off the light?!" Your emotions are connected to your morals, so you can see how they definitely affect how you act. The next day, you'll remember to turn off the light because you don't want to feel guilty again.

What Is Human Behavior?

The second part of this factor is culture, and it's pretty easy to see how culture changes how a person acts. From a young age, culture is ingrained in us, which affects us as we grow. That's why different cultures act differently. It's how they were raised.

The last factor is attitude. According to psychology, attitude is an expression of like or dislike toward something, somewhere, someone, or something that's happened. This is where we are all really unique. Everyone has different attitudes toward different things. For one, I love peanut butter. I happen to think it's the best thing ever. My friend, on the other hand, hates it. I know, you guys, it's shocking! Who could hate peanut butter? My friend, that's who.

So when some angel in a bakery offers me a sample of a chocolate peanut butter cake, I die and go to heaven (like most of us would). However, my friend gets all weird and then starts looking around the bakery, distrustful of any baked good like they are all going to have peanut butter in them. Because my attitude is in favor of peanut butter and hers is not in favor of it, we have completely different reactions to the bakery.

Attitudes can bring people together or tear them apart. Obviously, if my friend and I had different attitudes on everything, we probably wouldn't be friends. Thankfully, we only disagree on our love and hate for peanut butter. The way we all behave depends on how we perceive a situation at hand and what we expect to gain or lose from it. Because of this, our behavior is greatly affected by attitude.

> **Key Takeaways:**
>
> - Human behavior must be understood so that we can change.
> - Genetics can affect our behavior and patterns, but it isn't the only thing responsible.
> - Social norms make individuals act in a way that is closely aligned with the group.
> - Everyone is creative, and creativity shows in our behaviors every day.
> - Faith, morals, and culture affect us from the time we are young through adulthood.
> - Our attitudes about everything will determine the behavior we exhibit.

Even when some of us are faced with certain death, we have a hard time changing. According to a study done by Deutschman, only 9% of heart disease patients changed their lifestyle after they had a sever bypass surgery. These people were told they would die if they didn't change, but still, less than 1/10 of them did.

So, why is it so hard for us to change?

UCLA professor Matt Lieberman talks about the brain being divided into the X-system and C-system. The

What Is Human Behavior?

X-system reacts immediately, reacts fast, and is very energy-efficient. The C-system reacts more slowly and reflects higher-order thinking. Its job is to keep the X-system in check, challenge it, and even correct it if it's wrong.

Most of what we do throughout the day requires no thinking. Brushing your teeth and driving your car is all done by the X-system. This is so that the C-system can spend time processing new information and making decisions.[6]

We all have a hard time changing because it takes a while. It requires more energy and effort to think about doing something new than it does to do something out of instinct or habit. Our brains also have an error alert, so it notifies us when something happens that is out of the ordinary from what we'd expect. Like when your house creaks and you know you're the only one home, your brain starts to work overtime and sends an error because there could be an intruder. However, once you realize that it's just the water passing through the pipes, your brain should go back to normal. Your brain doesn't like change or the unexpected happening. When you try to change something, your brain is going to set off that error alert because it's not what it is used to.

Change feels threatening, and our brains are programmed to avoid threatening situations and embrace familiar systems with reward. Threats give us negative emotions and don't allow us to focus, whereas rewards give us positive emotions and release dopamine (the happy chemical) into our brains.

Evolve Your Habits

All in all, our brain hates to change. Thankfully, though, it's not impossible even if I've made it sound that way. Our brains are equipped with neuroplasticity, which means the brain will literally change its physical structure and function based on the experiences, behaviors, and emotions you are experiencing.[7]

You have to change your brain, and unfortunately, this can take a while. We are used to hearing the saying that it takes 21 days to break a habit. Actually, it can be shorter or much longer, depending on what you're trying to change. For example, reaching for an old toothbrush instead of your new one might take you a few days to change. But becoming sober from alcohol or drugs could take months or years to accomplish.

Regardless of what you're trying to change, *start small*. Don't use up all your willpower by trying to change everything at once. To become spontaneous, don't skip straight to skydiving. Try taking a different route to work, ordering something different at your favorite coffee shop, etc.

Another tip to help change is to *pay attention to the changes you are making.*

When you get distracted, you go back to old habits. Every time you make a change, notice it, because that old habit is becoming weaker. You should also try to reduce your stress. Practicing mindfulness is a great way for this to happen, but if that's not your thing, try exercising, getting out with friends, and getting the sleep that you need. These activities could help increase your serotonin, which will increase your willpower.

One of the things that will really help you change is to *avoid the triggers of your old behavior*.

If you want to become more spontaneous and stop binge-watching so much TV, try spending more time outside away from the screen. Sitting indoors would be like trying to be best friends with your trigger—it won't help.

And finally, *celebrate all the victories*. When you do something out of the ordinary and step out of your comfort zone, reward yourself. Celebrate that you did it, and be happy no matter how small of a victory it was.

> **Key Takeaways:**
>
> - Your brain is going to try to get you to stick to your old ways due to the systems in place.
> - Change is hard, threatening, and can be scary because of how our brain works.
> - Change is not impossible due to our brain's neuroplasticity.
> - To change, you need to focus on what you're doing and accept that it will take a while.
> - Focus on starting small and celebrating the changes you are making.

3

What Is Behavioral Change?

Even when we are young, a lot of us think we are old. We get to our teenage years and feel like adults. When we are in our 20s, we start worrying about life not happening. Our 30s are focused on our careers and/or families. 40s come, and we feel over the hill. 50s come, and we think we're officially old, but then we reach our 60s, 70s, 80s, and 90s. And yet when you're in your 20s, you think the teens are young, just like the 50-year-olds who think that those in their 30s are young, and those in their 70s are going to think that those in their 50s are really young.

No matter what our age, we often make up excuses not to change because we are too busy or too old. Elderly folks often resist change because it's been in their nature for so long. There are those who are in their 80s and still smoking a pack of cigarettes a day and refuse to quit because they think they are too old. But you're never too old to change!

What Is Behavioral Change?

Changes in behavior sometimes just happen, and other times we have to work really hard on things. In our day to day lives, it might seem that nothing is changing, but we look back at a year or five years ago and we see a drastic change in what our life was like then and the person we are now. We change based on time, experiences, and our impulses.

We all might think that we know what behavior change is, but it actually goes much in depth than just a few changes here and there. It can be a habit change, but it can also be consistent actions that will change, or us improving on ourselves. Maybe it's awareness or consciousness about the self. In reality, behavior change is changing our viewpoint and our circumstances together. You can't do one without the other and expect a behavior to really change.

It should come as no surprise then that there are a lot of theories in psychology about what behavioral change is and what spurs it. However, there are a few main theories that many of us know a thing or two about. These scientific theories have been studied time and time again and encompass the different ways we all change our behavior.

Classical Conditioning[8]

The first theory is called classical conditioning, but you might know it more by the person who studied it, Pavlov.

Pavlov worked with dogs, dog food, and a bell to measure the response these dogs had. Every time he gave the dogs the food, he would ring a bell. It was important to ring the bell right after he handed the food over to the dogs. Pavlov would study how the dogs would salivate for the food. Over time, the dogs began salivating just for the sound of the bell because they learned that the bell would signal the presence of food.

Pavlov's findings basically mean that a conditioned stimulus like the food is paired with an unconditioned stimulus like the bell, and the response then happens with the unconditioned stimulus over time.

John B. Watson did another example of classical conditioning. He conditioned a boy to become fearful of a white rat. At first, the little boy wasn't afraid of the rat, but then the rat was paired with a very loud clanging sound. The response to this sound was the little boy was afraid. Over time, the little boy became fearful of the white rat because he was fearful of the clanging noise that came with the animal. So if you have a fear, which we all do, it could have been formed because you had a bad experience with it.

We form our fears or our phobias because we want to survive. Even if the fear is silly, like maybe you're afraid of bouncy houses, it can be your brain's way of keeping you alive. A child who was almost trampled and broke their arm in a bouncy house might forever be afraid of bouncy houses.

This can even happen with animals and food. One famous study dealt with sheep and coyotes. Coyotes were eating the sheep of ranchers, so they developed a poison to inject into sheep carcasses that would make coyotes sick. It wouldn't kill them, but it caused the coyotes to have such a strong aversion to the sheep that they would not eat them, and some of them wouldn't even come near sheep any longer.

Operant Conditioning[9,10]

Another theory that talks about how behaviors change is B.F. Skinner's Operant Conditioning theory. It says that behaviors that are reinforced will continue, but behaviors that are punished will end. This is different than classical conditioning because the response is voluntary, rather than involuntary.

It's like if you study for a difficult test and get a good grade, you're more likely to study next time. Or if you make your favorite pasta dish and everyone likes it, you're more likely to make that dish again when your friends come over. But if you decide to go out and drink eight shots of tequila before your seven a.m. exam and flunk it, you're probably not going to do that again on an exam night.

It's a theory that is based on positive and negative reinforcement. Positive reinforcers are when good outcomes happen, like a reward or praise. Negative reinforcers are removing an unwanted outcome once the behavior happens. The goal for these reinforcers is to have the behavior increase.

On the other hand, there is also positive and negative punishment in this theory. Positive punishment is when unfavorable outcomes are given after a behavior. Negative punishment is when a favorable outcome is removed after the behavior. The goal in both punishments is to have the behavior decrease in frequency.

For example, positive reinforcement happens when your boss compliments your work after you turn in a project. On the other hand, negative reinforcement would happen when you turn in a work project and your boss tells you that if you do well on the next assignment, he'll assign a project no one wants to your coworker instead of you. The outcome is still good, but something is being taken away rather than added.

Now, punishment happens when the behavior is supposed to decrease. So the positive punishment would be adding something that's not fun after the behavior happens. This could be that your boss criticizes you when you do something incorrectly. Negative punishment would be like if your boss took away the promotion you were expected to get because you did the work wrong.

Tiny Habits[11]

Tiny Habits is a program that was developed by B.J. Fogg, who is a professor at Stanford University. He's been featured many times in different books and magazines, and he's had his own TED Talk, so it's safe to say his way of creating new behaviors in your life actually works. It lies in changing your environment and taking baby steps.

Imagine you want to run a marathon. Do you suddenly sign up for a marathon that is happening next week when you can barely run one mile without collapsing? That seems ridiculous, but we try to do that when we make changes! It's actually comical how we try to change our behaviors, because we rush into things and it becomes this huge ordeal.

Instead, we need to take tiny steps and celebrate each small step that we take immediately after doing it. In addition to that, your environment needs to change. If you want to eat healthier, you can't keep all the donuts and pastries in your cabinet. Instead, you have to throw those out, buy healthy foods, and voilà, your environment is changed! Unfortunately, it isn't always as easy as throwing away the donuts. Some behaviors are going to be harder to change the environment of, but you should try to change it as best as you can.

The next step is taking your tiny steps. The reason this works is that you're not exerting your willpower too much. Also, if you start small, the habit gets created. B.J. mentioned that he desired to do 70 pushups a day. However, he had no upper body strength, so he started small. Every time he would go to the bathroom, he would do two pushups. Once that became easier, he went to five pushups, then eight pushups. He created the habit of doing pushups after going to the bathroom, so now it comes naturally.

By starting small and committing to doing this small thing every day, you create a small habit that actually works. Plus, who is going to give up on doing two pushups? It's easy! And once these habits are in place in your life, they are going to be hard to break, which is a good thing. Soon enough, you have a long-term behavior change that you can be proud of.

Cognitive Behavioral Therapy

Cognitive Behavioral Therapy has become very popular in recent years because it's a psychotherapy that focuses on solutions, rather than root cause. Maybe you have a horrible habit that you want to break. Traditional therapy would try to understand why that habit is in place. This can take a long time, and it's often not that successful in actually changing the habit. On the other hand, CBT works on finding a solution. Do you have an alcohol addiction? While some therapists may work through your childhood to find out your father was also an alcoholic, CBT is going to ask you what you can do to change this behavior and find a solution.

It works by encouraging patients and challenging what you already think you know. What we do know is often distorted, and we tend to have a bias against ourselves.

CBT challenges that and tries to change these destructive patterns. By changing this unhelpful thinking, CBT works to make patients happier and healthier.

This therapy is shorter than most, as it usually takes under a year, but it is done in an office with a psychologist or therapist. It's revered for its ability to truly change behavior, and if you have something you want to change that might be too difficult for you to do alone, this is a great way to get it finally out of your life.

Stages of Behavioral Change

I'm just going to briefly mention this theory because the whole next chapter is going to be dedicated to it. You might know this as the Stages of Change Model or the Transtheoretical Model of Behavior Change. This theory states that there are five stages that we go through before achieving a final change.

The five stages are precontemplation, contemplation, preparation for action, action, and maintenance. During precontemplation, you may or may not be aware of the problem you have, but either way, you don't have any plans to change it. During contemplation, you start to finally think about changing the behavior you don't like. Preparation stage is when you're planning to change, action means you are actually changing, and maintenance means that you have the new behavior down pat and have been doing it for over six months. The only problem here is that sometimes people relapse after the maintenance stage, and this theory doesn't take that into account.

> **Key Takeaways:**
>
> - Classical conditioning works with conditioned stimuli and unconditioned stimuli to create the desired response.
> - Operant conditioning uses punishment and reinforcements to change an unwanted behavior and develop a wanted behavior.
> - Tiny Habits is a new behavioral change technique that works by taking small steps to create unbreakable habits.
> - Cognitive Behavioral Therapy is an in-office therapy that creates a better mood and works toward a solution to a problem.
> - The Stages of Behavioral Change model has five different stages that we go through when making a change, but some people still relapse.

4
The Transtheoretical Model

All of us have failed at making a change before. If you don't think you have failed, let me just leave you with three words: New Year's resolutions.

Yep, all of us have a failed resolution that we lovingly made on the first of January. While our intentions were good, we just didn't follow through. Now, that doesn't mean that all of your resolutions have failed. There's a good chance that you've also had some positive and successful changes in your life, including New Year's resolutions!

But let's be honest... Change is hard. Change can be painful. And there isn't one method that works for everyone. Hell, sometimes we need multiple methods for the same person just to work through different issues! When I wanted to eat healthier, I had to try to change in a different way than when I wanted to start working out. Even though they were somewhat of the same category of change, I needed to use two different ways to try and get there.

However, this is where the Stages of Change model is really helpful. When we understand the elements and stages of change, we have a much easier time trying to actually change. There are three important elements to change, and that's *your readiness, your barriers, and your relapse*.

I know, I know, none of us wants to relapse, but we should expect it to happen. With our readiness to change, we need to ask ourselves if we have everything we need to change. Are we knowledgeable in what we are changing, do we have access to the necessary resources, etc.? Thinking of these things before we start trying to change makes the change more successful in the long run.

Now, with the barriers to change, you have to ask yourself what is currently out there that's preventing you from changing. It could be a person, a thing, or even an event. And now with your relapse, come up with a list of things that could trigger you to return to that behavior.

So, for example, let's say you want to eat healthier. You'd ask yourself and answer questions like these:

Readiness: Do I have everything I need to make this lasting change?

Yes, I have stocked up on healthy foods and recipes for all my meals and snacks throughout the day.

Barriers: What could prevent you from eating healthy?

Sometimes my coworkers bring in donuts or treats to share in the office break room.

Expect Relapse: What could trigger me to eat unhealthily?

When my friends want to go out and grab drinks or brunch together.

These elements of change can be done with any habit you want to break.

Once you understand the elements of change, it's a lot easier to understand the well-known theory created by James Prochaska and Carlo DiClemente in the 1970s. It's called the Stages of Change model, and it was originally developed when looking at how to get individuals to stop smoking. Over time, it has become really helpful in understanding how human behavior changes.[12]

There are actually six stages of change in this model, and talking about each of them provides insight into how you can change your behavior, or why you haven't changed so far.

Precontemplation

The very first stage in this model is when you are unaware of the change needing to take place. It's like your friends might think you need to change the way you eat, but no one has said anything and you do not realize it yourself. People in this stage have zero interest in change and can't see the need for it. Also, they'll defend their behavior because they don't think it's an issue in their lives. As much as people try to convince a person like this that something needs to change, it's not going to happen while they are at this stage. You often hear the saying that you can't change people who don't want to change. It's true. Those people are in this precontemplation stage with no desire to change yet.

Contemplation

This is really the beginning of how a change happens. In this stage, a person actually knows (or admits) that there is a problem, and they think about changing it in the future. Knowing that their life could be better from changing this behavior is a big motivator. However, they are only considering change and have not committed to anything.

Think of this as the stage where you are going to weigh the pros and the cons of change. You're open to more information about changing your behavior and you're ready to decide whether or not you will change.

Preparation

Just like the word preparation, this stage is all about getting ready to actually change. It's when a commitment is made because the seriousness of the issue is recognized. Maybe someone finally realizes smoking is killing them, or they want to change their diet so they aren't so tired all the time. Whatever it is, they have committed to change within the next few weeks. It's a planning stage, so there is definitely planning going on here. This stage is also considered to be the shortest because you're not making any action toward the change except the planning and preparation.

Action

People who are actively making a change to better their lives are at this stage. It's one of the hardest stages of change because the temptation to quit is so alluring. Since you haven't been doing the new behavior for too long, the chance of relapse is pretty high. It's not a habit you have made permanent, but it is definitely getting there. A person can expect to stay in this stage for about six months until they move onto the next stage.

Maintaining

After about six months of action, you might be able to breathe a bit better and enter the maintenance stage. While relapse is still a temptation, this stage is all about resisting that temptation. There is a lower chance of relapsing because you have been doing this new behavior for quite some time and it's now become a big part of your life. Reaching out to similar people can help prevent relapse, which is why alcoholics often go to group meetings like Alcoholics Anonymous. Reminding yourself of the progress you have made is important at this stage.[13]

Termination

This sixth stage was not developed by the original researchers, but added more recently to try and build on their work. In this stage, the person doesn't have a desire to go back to any of the old habits they have now broken. Their new behavior feels so natural that going back would be strange.

Benefits of the Model

There has been some talk about the effectiveness of this model (which I'll talk about in just a little bit), but there are a lot of benefits that come from working with this model and understanding how a person goes through these stages. These are called the ten processes of change.

One benefit is that this model raises awareness. It is consciousness-raising because a person is going out there to get the facts of what's going on with their own behavior. Educating yourself is never a bad thing, so this model is a great way to get real feedback about what you are doing and which stage you are in.

Another process of change is called dramatic relief. What this means is that people who work through these stages of change pay more attention to their feelings and what's going on with them. When they feel fear and anxiety, they start to worry about their behavior. On the other hand, they'll also feel hope when they hear about

The Transtheoretical Model

people similar to them being able to change.

This model can also help reevaluate yourself and your priorities. When you notice a behavior you don't like and want to change, you are determining that the new behavior works with your self-image you want to create. You're making yourself better and creating a new and healthier image.

It's no secret that we are a bit biased with ourselves, so environmental reevaluation, or noticing the effect we have on others, is another positive effect this change model can bring about. For example, if a mother realizes that their alcoholism is affecting their child's outcomes, they can change.

Social liberation can also come from this model, and it happens when you realize that society is much more supportive of a healthier behavior. People are much more supportive of a smoker who is trying to quit than a smoker who doesn't care if they are blowing smoke in their friends' faces.

Making a commitment to yourself is considered to be self-liberation, and it shows just how much you can believe in yourself. Recognizing that this change is possible and believing you can be better and do better will help you make even more changes in the future.

Creating new relationships, or finding old supportive ones, is helpful to your change, and it's another benefit of this model. You reach out and find people who are going to be supportive of your desire to change.

Counter-conditioning and substituting your unhealthy

behavior for healthy ones is a benefit to this way of changing.

The Stages of Change model also helps with rewards and reinforcement management. It means that you are going to celebrate the victories more, and you're going to punish the behaviors that are not conducive to your new change.

Last, but not least, this model helps with stimulus control and managing your environment. The supporters of this model talk about encouraging every healthy behavior and not encouraging the unhealthy behavior. This might mean you use reminders or small cues throughout your change process to help you change in a better way.

Limitations of the Model

As much as this theory is revered and loved, there are a few limitations that should be considered when understanding it. Change isn't black and white, so there isn't going to be one single solution that is going to change everything for you. It's hard to determine where a person is at in the stages, because it's not like there is a set criterion to determine it. There are a few tests a person can take, but they aren't validated by science.

Plus, we don't know how long each person should stay in each stage. Some people might take a long time in the contemplation stage while others take longer in the action stage. We assume when using this model that everyone is making logical plans, but that's not always the case. It wasn't a logical decision when I moved to Germany, and yet it still happened. Humans aren't always logical, so the stages of change can be even more blurred when taken that into account.

And finally, another limitation is that this model doesn't take into account social contexts like income and socioeconomic status. Other change models do consider this because it is often a determining factor in whether or not people change. For example, people in a lower socioeconomic class that don't have any healthy grocery stores nearby are going to have a much harder time staying healthy than someone in a high socioeconomic class who is surrounded by stores with healthy options.

Key Takeaways:

- The Stages of Change model is a helpful tool that can help you understand how and when you are changing.
- There is always the risk of relapsing, but the deeper into the stages you go, the less likely that is.
- The end goal is for the old behavior to feel foreign and strange after going through the stages of change.
- This model has 10 processes of change that can be considered very beneficial.
- There are still some limitations, like lack of criteria and social context ignorance.

5

Why Do You Resist Change?

When I was a little girl, I was riding in the car with my grandmother. She told me how important it is to eat your fruits and vegetables, and I definitely agreed with her. However, being the small child I was, I asked her why she ate so many desserts. I laugh now, because I mean, what grandma doesn't eat a ton of desserts?

She laughed as well and then answered with, "Well, my advice is still good. Just do as I say and not as I do." And that's what so many of us say. We have no problem telling our friend who smokes that they are giving themselves cancer, but when someone tells us about the importance of exercise we brush them off.

So, here's the thing: No one is questioning that changing a bad behavior is more beneficial. We know that quitting smoking, eating healthier, exercising more, stressing less, balancing our work and personal life, and managing our money better would be more beneficial to our lives. We know all of this.

But knowing doesn't substitute us doing. And that's the hardest part. We aren't the most logical species, but that's actually helped us in our evolution. We often think abstractly, and logic just isn't our brain's best friend. Instead, we resist all change, even though we know it's better for us. Why do we do it?

I'm going to talk about the reasons why this happens, but I'm splitting it into three different categories: reasons we are aware of, reasons we are unaware of, and external aspects.

Reasons We Are Aware Of

We are actually aware of a lot of the reasons why we don't like to change. I bet if I asked you to list some, you would probably have a few reasons that you are not willing to change. Actually knowing these reasons can help you go above and beyond them so that you can change later on.

It should come as no surprise that one of the biggest reasons we resist changing is because of low self-esteem. We're always saying things like, "I just can't do it," or "I'm not good enough." It's a mentality that a lot of us have, but allow me to let you in on a secret… It doesn't help us at all! We compare ourselves negatively to others, and that makes us feel horrible. And because we feel horrible, our self-esteem then goes down even more. I used to be guilty of comparing myself to others based on their social media posts. You know what I'm talking about, that person who has the perfect feed and is always traveling with their perfect boyfriend who loves them so much that they are always receiving flowers and gifts. They're living the life, right?

Actually, no. Social media is another person's highlight reel. We are comparing our worst moments to their highlights. Just knowing that these people aren't perfect and that they have hardships like the rest of us helped my self-esteem a lot.

Another reason that we resist change comes from our own self-hatred. It's the mentality that you are bad and that you have a low self-worth. You think that changing yourself is a waste of time because you don't deserve it. This is a real issue, and it's worse than low self-esteem because it means you have low expectations for your life.

A high pain tolerance can cause you to resist change as well. Perhaps your partner cheated on you. Even though you know that it's not okay, you might say that you are used to the pain and would feel worse if you gave up the relationship. Maybe you hate your job, but going without a job while searching for something you like isn't what you want to do. While endurance and resilience are good qualities, they are not good when they become self-destructive. Denying pain or being overly optimistic will actually hurt you in the end. Sometimes things don't get better, and that means you have to move on.

Another reason to avoid change we are all familiar

with is that we have a fear of failure and confrontation. No one wants to feel stupid, and sometimes change brings about that judgment. When I went to Germany, my father literally threatened to cut me off and give away my inheritance because he thought my decision was crazy. I experienced intense fear as I started thinking that maybe I really was making an irreversibly bad decision. I didn't want to tell my father, and when I finally did, his reaction was hurtful. When fear is so intense, it can convince a person not to change at all. They believe that failure is a guaranteed outcome of trying to change, so their fear stops them from even attempting.

All of these fears of failing, being rejected, or being wrong, are emotional experiences that we have had in the past. But guess what? So has everyone else. These emotions are so deeply ingrained that they are part of our primal makeup. Instead of getting hurt, we don't act at all. To change, we have to learn to become masters of our own fears. I find that when I stop worrying about what might happen, I feel a lot better. Also, I have a tendency to generalize. When something goes wrong, then everything else goes wrong. However, that's not true. Being aware of your generalizations can help you. Lastly, avoiding labels and stopping the obsession of being accepted can help you get over all of these reasons for resisting.

Reasons We're Unaware Of

Reasons we resist change that we are unaware of can be the most damaging to us. These reasons are often embedded into our brains during our childhood, and we don't realize that we are doing them until someone or something points it out. It usually takes CBT to realize these deeply rooted problems so that we can move past them.

One of the biggest factors is our negative self-talk. While this is similar to self-esteem, it's different because it is part of our personality and we don't realize we are doing it. When our self-esteem interferes, our brain knows that it is wrong. When we are saying things like, "I'm not that type of person," or, "I'm not competing in a math competition because only losers go," our brain doesn't try to tell us that we are wrong.

We all have a bit of negative self-talk, but sometimes the problem is so severe that we literally cannot change because of it. Negative self-talk demands to be obsessed about, and it forces our body to believe whatever is supposed to fit in our story. Maybe we get hurt because a date doesn't end up showing up at the restaurant. Instead of recognizing the hurt, the negative self-talk would justify it by saying something like, "It's okay she ditched me because relationships are dumb and too time-consuming, anyhow."

Another issue we are dealing with are past traumas. Even when we think we might be "over" an issue, it can still affect our subconscious desires and actions. It's

Why Do You Resist Change?

the mindset of, "I've been burned before, and I'm not going to be burned again." Different experiences leave their fingerprints on our decision-making later on in life. If you were bitten by a dog as a child and had to get stitches, you might choose to never own a dog or even go near one. Or maybe you once had a woman boss who hated you, so you subconsciously avoid any job that has a woman boss. Sometimes, we don't even know why we react a certain way to someone. It's the classic "what the hell was I thinking?" scenario.

Different things can trigger responses in our subconscious. We decide to react in the way that worked for us before in the past. An easy example of this would be like how you react to bees. Some of us jump and run away because we know it hurts to be stung and running away will prevent that. On the other hand, some people just sit and don't worry about it. Most of those people haven't been stung, or if they have, it wasn't a traumatic experience.

A reason that is very popular among all of us in resisting change is our fixed mindsets. We simply say that we already know, and we aren't going to be able to change that. It's like if I asked you to bake a cake from scratch without a recipe. You'd probably say you couldn't (unless you are a baker), but if I asked you how you knew you couldn't bake a cake from scratch, your answer would be because you know you can't. And while this isn't detrimental when it comes to baking a cake, it can greatly affect us.

The fixed mindset was introduced by Carol Dweck, and it says that we think that traits are unchangeable and permanent. The only way to succeed in life is to prove that our existing traits are good.

On the other hand, there is growth mindset, which states that we can improve upon the traits we have. We know we can be smarter, work harder, be kinder, etc. This mindset is instilled in us at a young age, and the mindset we have will determine how we think about change. We either say, "I can't do that," or we say, "It's going to take work, but I know I can do it eventually."[14]

External Aspects

There are some circumstances we have thrust upon us, and it can affect how we think about change. One of these external aspects is a lack of education and resourcefulness. Now, I'm not talking about going to school. I'm talking about accessing data you are curious about and teaching yourself something new.

Another issue is having a harmful environment. If people are telling you that you can't or shouldn't do something, you might think you should believe them. The people closest to us can sometimes bring us down. It might be masked as caring for you, and they might not even know they are doing it, but it is still bringing you down. Maybe you avoid that one family member who always has a different opinion for you and is too stuck

Why Do You Resist Change?

in their ways to know. Perhaps you have a grandmother who believes that the only way for a family to succeed is with a man working and a woman staying at home. Whatever it is, these opinions are not always right and should not determine your life.

There's also restricting social norms because none of us like change. "If it ain't broke, don't fix it," is how the saying goes. These restricting norms are often typical in small communities, religious groups, or niche environments. If you want to be an insider, you have to comply with their rules. But sometimes, this need for belonging only harms us because we sacrifice our own wishes.

The excuse we all love to use, which is that we have no time for change, is also an external aspect. When you have a family of five, a full-time job, kids to care about, an unsupportive spouse, college courses, or dishes to wash, no one is thinking about change. We think that our obligations will go away at some point, but they never do. However, you probably overestimate the time you need. Most often, it only takes about 10 minutes of mindfulness and dedication to start a change. Everyone can make time for that.

Lastly, another reason is that we feel just fine where we are. Our lukewarm life conditions aren't inspiring us to change because the pond we're in isn't too hot and it's not too cold. It might not be good enough, but it's not bad enough, either. You do okay, your marriage is okay, and you have okay friends. Which is fine, if you're fine with it, but it's not going to make you want to improve. When something finally does change, people in these situations crumble because they are so unfamiliar with change itself.

Yes, change can hurt. Change can be hard and annoying. It might even feel like your mother nagging you back when you were in elementary school. However, it is good for you. You probably have a combination of all of these reasons you don't want to change, but I can bet that deep inside, change is actually very enticing to you. I'll talk about that more in the next chapter.

> **Key Takeaways:**
>
> - We know change is good, but we often don't change regardless.
> - Low self-esteem, a high pain tolerance, and fears can prevent us from changing.
> - Sometimes, our past has a tight grip on us and prevents us from truly changing.
> - Our life conditions can also convince us change isn't wanted or needed.
> - We have the ability to change, despite what we think or tell ourselves.

6

Why'd You Buy This Book?

There are a million reasons why someone doesn't want to change, but people still change every day. There has to be some part of us that deep down actually wants to change, right? I can bet that you want to change something in your life, or you wouldn't have bought this book. Since you did, let's talk about you changing.

First things first, I want you to think about what motivates you. What are the things that are pushing you to change? Think about it all and then write it down. This is just the beginning. While motivation is a great start, it won't get you too far on your road to behavioral change.

The reason for this is because your motivation is limited, just like your willpower is. It's going to run out quickly, so if you rely solely on motivation, you're going to sink like you're in quicksand. Sure, motivation will keep you going for a bit, as will willpower, but psychologists are now on the side of these being limited resources.

We used to think that willpower was unlimited. We could delay gratification, as long as our willpower was strong. Resisting things comes naturally to us, and so there's no reason to think that willpower is limited. In 1998, Roy Baumeister conducted a study with two groups of people. One group ate cookies and the other group ate radishes. They found that the group who ate cookies could focus longer on a geometric task than the ones who ate radishes. The reason? Their willpower wasn't depleted.[15]

Willpower depletion has been studied numerous times since then, and it's been shown that your brain actually functions differently when expending willpower. It doesn't perform as well, so you end up suffering because of it. While we can resist temptation, our willpower gets depleted, so we have a harder time resisting the next temptation that is put in our path.

Willpower and your behavior have a relationship that is pretty cozy. We all like to say that we emotionally eat, but studies have shown that we emotionally eat when our willpower is depleted, not when we are experiencing an emotional high or low. In the case of behaviors like drugs or alcohol, exerting your willpower might work at first, but it can influence your decision-making afterward. Studies had shown that those who limited their alcohol intake in a controlled environment drank more when they were asked to sample alcohol, versus the group who did not have to exercise their self-control in the first drinking round.

Why'd You Buy This Book?

Willpower is a good thing, and it's our ability to resist that short-term gratification for a longer-term benefit. This is important when you're trying to change. It's related to positive life outcomes, but when willpower fails, it leads to a person being impulsive. Just like how our muscles become tired when we work out too hard, willpower can be overexerted as well. But showing self-control a little bit at a time can actually strengthen your willpower in the long run.

So just like willpower won't guarantee you are going to change, motivation won't, either. However, motivation can be the thing that jumpstarts you into making a change. We are aware of positive emotions being a motivator to us. When we are happy or experiencing love and success, it can help motivate us in the right direction. However, if that's all that was needed to make a change, we'd all be so satisfied in life that I wouldn't be writing this book.

There are also motivators that we aren't aware of, and they are often negative drivers which aim to help us feel better. So while we pursue happiness and are aware of it, trying to avoid unhappiness is unconscious, but something we all do.

And often, our insecurities can try to preserve our ego and happiness by trying to impress others. It's a cyclical process that happens to almost everyone you know. The university student tries to impress the teacher, the teacher tries to impress the dean, the dean tries to impress the university students with their shiny new sports car, etc.

It's a circle of deception because we want to be better than others, but even if we work hard to be better, we still feel like these people look down on us. So we push even harder, and it ends up hurting us in the long run.

Cognitive Dissonance[16]

A lot of this can be attributed to what's called cognitive dissonance.

Cognitive dissonance happens when there are conflicting ideas in our minds. We try to bridge the gap between these ideas, but it's not beneficial to us. For example, maybe you had a very strict upbringing, but you want to go out and party. You might bridge these two thoughts by convincing yourself that your parents did the same at your age.

We have an idea of who we are, but it doesn't always line up with reality. We end up avoiding cognitive dissonance, and that can be painful. Most of us view ourselves as good, and we think that we go out of our way to do good things. And maybe we do. It's like when you know your neighbor doesn't respect you, but you still offer to help them out all the time. Or when you are tired but your roommate says you have to go out to a party with them, you use your willpower and you get it done, but it eventually crumbles.

You get tired of being your version of Mother Teresa, so the next time someone asks, you rudely reject them. But you don't feel bad about it. Instead, you'll use cognitive dissonance and say something like, "I'm kind, and this rejection is actually showing that I am because now my neighbor is going to become more independent."

We rationalize, but this only stops our change because we come up with excuses. There are other motivators that will get us going, and they are the most obvious ones because we gain something or lose something from them. It still comes down to these motivators not being enough for you, at some point.

Think of money, status, or power. People lie and cheat to gain them, so they are very powerful motivators. But at some point, you'll have enough money, enough status, or enough power. There is nothing wrong with wishing for these things, but you have to know that you honestly value them.

There is also a survival instinct of motivation. We might seek validation or love from those around us. It can go a lot further than hoping your boss likes you, and it could be something like making sure your family is provided for and feeling validated that you are doing this for them. Unfortunately, this motivator can attract social anxiety and fear of not being enough. We want social acceptance. It's ingrained in our behavior to try and stay within the group, and this is something that has been studied and revered for a long time, otherwise known as Maslow's hierarchy of needs.

Maslow's Pyramid of Needs[17]

Maslow's pyramid goes through basic needs to more complex needs, and if your basic needs are not fulfilled, you cannot fulfill the complex ones.

The most basic needs of Maslow's hierarchy are physiological needs like oxygen, food, water, and sleep. It should come as no surprise that these have to be fulfilled before you can worry about other things. If you are not breathing or you are starving, that's going to take up all of your attention.

Once those needs are met, the next level is safety. This includes having the security of a job and other resources, having a family, being healthy, and having a place to stay. This doesn't necessarily mean that you are having great relationships; it just means that everything you have is safe and you don't need to worry about it.

The next level of the pyramid is love and belonging. This includes family, friends, and sexual intimacy. We all want to feel cared about, and it's the basis of our lives, once our physiological and safety needs are met.

The following level is esteem, and this includes your confidence, achievement, respect of others, others respecting you, and your self-esteem. The higher up in the pyramid you get, the more complex the needs get. When you have these needs met, you should feel very good and can make your way to the final stage.

The most complex need in Maslow's hierarchy is what's called reaching self-actualization. Psychologists focus on it a lot, and it's where everyone hopes to be. It deals with creativity, morality, problem-solving, lack of prejudice, and acceptance.

When you are deprived of any of these needs, it causes a lot of psychological problems. A deprivation of needs at any level of the pyramid can be distressing, but it is especially distressing when it occurs in the lower levels of the hierarchy.

All of these needs can be considered motivators, so it's easy to see that they are pushing us toward behavior. Perhaps you get a bad bill of health, so your motivator to get healthy would be fixing your heart issue, or whatever it is. But, as I mentioned in an earlier chapter, even when we know what we should be doing, we don't always do it.

In the next chapter, we are going to talk about what actually works.

Key Takeaways:

- Motivation and willpower will only get you so far if you want to change.
- There are a lot of motivators that we are aware of, and some that we are even unaware of.
- While they can start change in us, at some point the motivator won't be enough.
- It's not enough for just our basic and primal needs to be met.
- According to Maslow's hierarchy of needs, the complex needs to be met as well for the best self.

7

How Do You Start Changing?

Now that I've pretty much made making a change in your life sound impossible, I'm here to tell you why it is actually very possible. The reason that so many people don't change for good is that they don't know their "why." Your "why" is the reason that you want to make the change. It's important for you to think of the beliefs you hold, because these beliefs can often prevent you from changing and finding an alternate point of view.

First Steps to Change

We're going to do an exercise where you ask yourself the questions below and answer them. Think of the thing in your life that you want to change and ask yourself whether or not that's possible with these questions.

- What are your goals when engaging in this behavior? What are you getting out of it?

- What do I need to do to stop this behavior?
- What do those around me think about my behavior? Does it enable it to continue, or to stop?
- How do I know I can stop this?
- Where am I going when I act on this behavior?
- Can I resist temptation and delay gratification of this behavior?
- Do I need to do this, or do I just like doing the behavior?
- What could replace this bad behavior?
- Describe how this behavior happens on an ongoing basis.
- How does this behavior contribute to my self-image?[18]

After you've asked yourself these questions, you can create a new change in your life. Questioning your motivation and your old behavior helps you to realize how it limits you.

Stop the Procrastination

Procrastination is a natural behavior we all participate in. We just like to postpone things until it's the last minute. I'm a victim of this behavior! Seriously, I procrastinate way too often, and it doesn't ever help me. However, postponing things isn't the only way procrastination can present itself.

For perfectionists, I've got some news. If you are constantly trying to make everything perfect, you may struggle with being a perfectionist. This is actually a form of procrastination, because you wait until the perfect moment to change your bad behaviors. That day may never come! It stops you from taking action, and it's a relentless process of preparation. Because of this, procrastination is a symptom of being a perfectionist. You have the fear that the outcome won't be perfect, so you never take the action to begin with. Unlike the lazy connotation that comes with procrastination, perfectionists are not lazy; they just want to work *too* well.

Change is a messy process, so you have to accept that it isn't going to be perfect. The road to change is a dirt road that has divots and potholes. There is failure, hardship, and sometimes there is even pain. But guess what? That's okay! This road is the road to change, no matter what it looks like.

Perfection is unattainable, and being afraid of change because of what others think of you means that you are in a stage of resistance. You have to realize that there's a difference between perfection and personal excellence. While personal excellence is aiming to become the best version of yourself, perfection is trying to achieve the impossible. You can still achieve personal excellence if you eat a donut while trying to lose weight. You can still achieve personal excellence if you replace the addiction of smoking with running. And you can still achieve personal excellence if you quit your job without having another option lined up! Nothing needs to be perfect.

The funny thing is, even though we like to procrastinate, we also love to plan. Some of you might be list-makers, while others may not be. However, you don't need a mile-long list of how you are going to change your behavior. Don't fall prey to the trap of never-ending planning! You shouldn't deter your moment of action just because you don't have the most thought-out plan in the universe.

If you love to plan and it's a form of security, it's okay to indulge. But don't use planning as an excuse to not take action. You don't need to pick up 10 more books on behavior change before you can actually change. Give it at least a month of action before you try some other plan.

Set SMART Goals[19]

If you know the reason you want to change and you have officially beat procrastination, then it is time to do a little bit of planning. I know, I know, I just talked about *not* planning, but this is just a low-key way to give you some direction in how you will change.

Everyone wants to set smart goals, but most of us don't set SMART goals. SMART is an acronym that will help you create the best goals possible. So, let's break down this acronym.

The S stands for specific. Your goal should be simple, make sense, and be significant in your life. You can answer a few questions that will help you create your specific goal.

- What is it that you want to accomplish?
- Why is your goal important?
- Who is going to be involved in your goal?
- Where will this goal happen?
- What resources do you have available to help you meet this goal?

The M stands for measurable. A goal is not a goal without being able to measure it. The killer of goals is generalizing them. Saying, "I want to get richer this year," is not a good goal. You won't ever be able to measure that. You want to be $1 richer? $1,000 richer? Or maybe even $1,000,000 richer? You've got to be able to measure your goal. Ask yourself how much, how many, and how will you know when it's accomplished.

The A stands for achievable. Obviously, your goal should be realistic. Saying you want to land on the moon this year is ridiculous unless you're a NASA astronaut. While your goal should be challenging and motivate you to reach it, it shouldn't be so challenging that it's never going to happen. Try asking yourself how you will be able to accomplish this goal. Is it realistic, based on your current life situations?

The R stands for relevant. This is where your "why" comes in. If the goal doesn't matter to you, you're not going to put your heart and soul into it. Is your goal worth your time? Is it the right time to act upon it? Are you the right person to reach this goal? Asking yourself these three simple questions can help you determine whether or not your goal is relevant.

The T stands for time. You need a target date for your goal so that there is a deadline to focus on. It should answer the question of when this goal should be accomplished by.

Now that you know what SMART stands for, let me show you an example of SMART goals when it comes to behavior change. Let's say you want to increase your vegetable consumption. Maybe you never eat your greens and it's been weighing on your mind recently (which it should—come on, eat your greens!).

If I make my goal as eat more vegetables, it's probably not going to happen because that's the vaguest goal in the world. So let's make this goal SMART, shall we?

A smarter goal would be to say, "I will increase my vegetable consumption to two cups each day by October 15th to help me become a healthier individual."

S: increase vegetables
M: two cups
A: more than a month to achieve
R: vegetables make you healthier
T: October 15th

Instead of just saying you're going to increase your vegetables, you say that you're going to increase them to

How Do You Start Changing?

two cups a day. It's specific, measurable, attainable because you are giving yourself more than just a day or two to achieve it, and it's relevant because vegetables make you healthier and you want to become healthy. Also, it's got a deadline because we said October 15th.

It may seem simple, but creating goals like this can really help you achieve them. It's like creating a little calendar event on your phone but in your mind! You will be better off knowing your goal because you know by just how much or how little you are not reaching it. You can measure this goal, and it's got a deadline for you. Therefore, no procrastinating!

Key Takeaways:

- We need to change our beliefs by asking a set of important questions that help us analyze the behavior we want to change.
- Humans love to procrastinate.
- Procrastination can take the form of perfectionism or planning, which are both excuses to not act.
- Planning a little isn't bad, but it shouldn't be a mile-long list.
- Rewriting your goals to be SMART will help you achieve your goals and keep you held accountable.

8

How Do You Eat an Elephant?

You know when you're so hungry you say you could eat a horse? But then you get to that all-you-can-eat buffet, and suddenly you're a bit shy and don't seem to be as hungry as you were exclaiming in the car? Sometimes, we are overwhelmed because the goal that we have is too large. We don't even start doing what we are supposed to be doing because we can't see the end in sight, we're too scared because the goal is supposed to take too long, we don't know where to begin, or we are dealing with some resistance like low self-esteem.

This brings us to our chapter title. In the end, nothing is going to change if you try to make it happen all at once. How do you eat an elephant? You certainly don't eat it all in one sitting. You need to break it down into much smaller portions the same way you need to break your goal down into smaller steps.

Let's say you have a yearlong goal. In fact, I encourage

it! If you have a yearlong goal, you have to break it down into 12 monthly sub-steps. Then you break the monthly steps into weekly ones. Then take your weekly goal and divide into four activities you can get done during the day. This way, your big goal is broken down into 12x4x7x4 steps. Yes, that's 1344 steps. It sounds scary, but the good news is you don't have to break it all down at once. It doesn't need to be a huge chunk of dream.

First, you need to have your goal. This is obviously the most important part of setting goals, right? Then you just need to have your approximate monthly goal breakdown and the weekly breakdown for the first month. After that, make a to-do list for the next day based on your first week's agenda. Everything else can be done as you go. You'll figure out your daily task list as you go through your week.

Your monthly tasks might change a little, which is why you are only setting approximate monthly goals in the beginning. You get to optimize your plans as you progress toward your large goal. And thankfully, you don't need to use your first draft. Even writers don't use their first draft to publish. If they did, you'd probably hate the books you read!

What's most important here is that you should make your execution plan quickly. Once you have that big goal in mind, you should work fast on breaking it down while it is all fresh. If you wait too long to do your goal breakdowns, the scarier your goal will become. The scarier your goal becomes, the less likely you are to do something about it.

Evolve Your Habits

We live in 2018, which means that there are a lot of tools out there to help you. Here are a few of my favorites:

The Google Trial

Google pretty much seems to run our lives, and whenever we have a question, we go and visit it. Thankfully, this can work to our advantage when it comes to goals.

Using as few keywords as possible, enter your goal into Google. You can put something like "losing weight first steps" or "getting better job how to." The results are going to vary wildly depending on your goal, and you might love them or hate them.

The good news is that you don't have to follow what it's saying. If you hate it, forget it! If you love it, try it out. It can give you a sense of direction when you start out. Sometimes it's that first step that's the hardest, and you might be stumped when trying to figure out how to divide your goal. That's why Google might become one of your best friends. Try it out and see what you find. If anything, it's just educating you and giving you more info!

Limited Time

Sometimes you need a little fire underneath your butt. Let's say that you have a very limited time to act on your goal every day. Maybe it's only 10 or 20 minutes a day. What would be the most important task to finish here?

What would you try to get done first? While you might have more time than just a few minutes, you might not. When you limit yourself to this time constraint, it really tells you what is and what isn't important to your goal. You could spend minutes doing another task that isn't even important, but if you put yourself in this scenario, you'll really narrow down what has to get done. Try out this technique and see where it gets you for a week or so.

Small-Step It

This is where you are going to tailor-make information you hear so that it makes more sense to you. I like to say that you're small-stepping for your shoe size. Whenever you hear information or advice, break it down to your best knowledge. We are all different, so advice is going to mean different things to different people.

For example, my friend is amazing at copywriting and can do it in 30 minutes. For me, it'll take at least a day and the quality won't be anywhere near as good as hers. Step one for her is writing marketing text. However, for me, that takes at least three steps. Don't feel bad for how long something takes you versus how fast someone else can do it.

Fill in the Gaps

When you create a goal, you might not know everything. Again, this isn't bad. I am a huge proponent of self-education, and this is the perfect time for you to showcase that! Maybe you are trying to get healthy, but you don't know a lot about what you can and can't eat. That's a legitimate concern, and it's something that you can familiarize yourself with after a bit of research. When you are making your daily tasks, save one of those tasks for research and studying. It's so important to continue learning more, and this information stays with you forever. Don't ever think that studying is a waste of your time. It can only make your goal outcomes that much better.

Key Takeaways:

- Our goals can scare us, so we need to break them down into smaller parts.
- You'll want your goal to be broken down into 12x4x7x4: 12 months, 4 weeks, 7 days, 4 tasks a day.
- Come up with your goal and then quickly make your plan, otherwise it will never get done.
- Use different resources to your advantage; we live in 2018!
- Take small steps and learn more about your goal; it can only help in the long run.

9
Two Key Activities for Lasting Change

Sometimes change doesn't stick. We can try hard to change, we can succeed, and then we end up relapsing, or we just stop the new behavior and forget about it like the old boxes underneath our bed. It's annoying to put so much work into something only to see it fail. Thankfully, there are two key activities I'll tell you about that can help your behavior change last for as long as you want or need.

Keep Your Momentum

Which is easier: letting a car roll, or starting and stopping every few moments? Let me give you a little hint. Imagine your car is on a hill… What will be easier? Just letting it roll.

Much like the car, it's easier for us to keep our momentum in behavior change. What this means is that you aren't giving up when times get hard. Even when there are adverse conditions, you shouldn't stop trying to change. And even if you are failing, make your best effort to rise each time and keep walking forward. Don't give up on your behavior change just because you hit a few bumps in the road. Remind yourself what your goal is with the behavior change and recall all the struggle you have gone through to achieve it.

We are human. We like to stop for a second, catch our breath, and have a Nutella pancake before going back to do the hard labor. But more often than not, we get stuck in the pancake shop. We never go back to the hard work field once we tasted the sweetness of easy resting. This is why it is so crucial to not stop. You can slow down, go just 0.01 mile per hour—but go.

For example, you don't have to work very hard each day to achieve your seven figures a year—but even when you slow down, do something little. Just answer three emails, or just write two pages in your book, or just do a five-minute workout. Don't let your brain and body forget what hard work is. Keep yourself a little bit uncomfortable in your comfort.

To be able to realistically keep up the momentum long-term requires to not burn yourself on maximum speed at the beginning. If you're pushing and pushing at your maximum force, you might make some progress, but then you'll fall off the bandwagon. That's not what you want to go! Settling for a normal speed and keeping

Two Key Activities for Lasting Change

your momentum is the way to not burn yourself out.

You don't always see the return on your behavior change, so it can be hard to know whether or not you are working on it. Because of this, your natural reaction is to push yourself even harder. But I have one word for you...

Chill.

Seriously, you just need to relax a little. One thing that helps a lot is keeping an accomplishment journal. Write down each day what progress you made toward your goal. This provides you with physical proof that the change is happening, even if you can't see it right in front of you. I suggest writing down three examples each day about the changes you have made.

Another thing that can help keep motivation going is knowing when to do something and knowing when to not do something. Don't just do it for the sake of doing it. Being busy does not mean that you are making progress. Sometimes, you think that you need to do more, and so you will do some useless activity that doesn't actually help you work toward your goal. It's better to do the important stuff and take the other time to do your normal day-to-day activities.

As humans, we often get bored, and this can affect our motivation. Mix up your routine so that you aren't doing the same thing over and over again. There is a theory in psychology that is called the Yerkes-Dodson Law. Developed by the two psychologists, this law aims to find the correct arousal level for optimal performance. It says that activities that require a lower level of arousal are often activities you need to focus and concentrate on, whereas activities that require stamina or perseverance need higher levels of arousal. Think of it like this: a calculus test requires a lot of focus, so you won't be too aroused. However, a soccer game requires stamina and excitement, so a higher level of arousal will lead to a better performance. Each person is different, and it often depends on the task at hand, but try to find your perfect level of arousal for the tasks that you are doing. This can help your motivation so that you aren't just wasting time and energy.[20]

There's also another law that you should follow, and that's Parkinson's Law. What this law says is that you have to find the right amount of time for each task. If you give yourself a week to complete an hour-long task, that work is going to fill up the whole week. Even if the work itself won't fill it up, the worry and anxiety knowing you have to finish it will fill up the week. To prevent that, you need to give yourself realistic deadlines. This can be difficult for us, so try the activity below.

First, create a list of all the tasks you need to get finished. Then divide them up according to the time it's going to take to finish them. Now give yourself half that time to finish them. Imagine that your deadlines are unbreakable. This might seem stressful, but it's actually beneficial, because you'll end up taking your own deadlines seriously.

This exercise also helps to determine how accurate your time projections for your tasks are. You can use a timer to time yourself on your tasks to see which time projections were right, which were too long, and which were too short.

Creating a schedule for yourself can also help you to get the work done. Even if you can only work for five minutes a few times a day, it's important to stick to the schedule because it builds a habit (which I'll talk about in the next chapter).

Finally, you should be ready to fail. Failure can help your motivation, and it's inevitable from time to time. It's the nature of life, and sometimes we have to hit rock bottom. The good news is that when we fail, we see where we can improve and grow stronger so you won't fail again at the same thing.

Follow-Up Feedback

Even if we change and progress at an impressive rate, it's always a good idea to do some follow-up and ask for feedback from the people around us. This can help us make corrections along the way. We don't always see where we have made mistakes, and evaluation from others can help us to see where we may have lacked in the heat of the moment.

However, feedback from others isn't the only way to get feedback. You can get a lot of feedback from yourself as well. First, you should listen to your body and your mind. This is going to give you feedback on whether or not you are physically on the right track. If you're always exhausted, you are less focused, your blood pressure is rising, or you're anxious, that means you're pushing yourself way too hard. One way to get your own body feedback is by checking your heart rate. Count how many times your heart is beating in 60 seconds. It should be anywhere between 60 and 100. If it's too fast or too slow, that isn't a good sign. You might be exposed to too much stress and pressure.

You should also look into your sleeping habits. We need anywhere from seven to eight hours of sleep, but many adults aren't getting that. Your quality of sleep also matters. If you're constantly getting disrupted or you're tossing and turning, it's a good indicator that your sleep could be a lot better. Try winding down before bed and creating a routine where you go to sleep and get up at the same time each day. This can help improve your sleep quality.

Another way to get feedback is by focusing on your focus. Try to say that five times fast! Seriously, though, when you are reading the same line over and over again, your brain clearly is distracted by something else. You're not fresh or alert, which means you probably need to step away from the task and do something to get your focus back. A few minutes of mindfulness, a walk around the office, or taking a breath of fresh air outside can help.

Two Key Activities for Lasting Change

A lot of research about monitoring yourself has been done by William J. Fremouw and John P. Brown, Jr. They talked about self-monitoring reactivity. When we monitor, reassure, and report the results of our change, we are more likely to change because we are being monitored. It works with both behaviors we want to increase and behaviors we want to decrease. It's one of the best ways to track behavior patterns and eventually change them, because you can see what triggers it and when it appears.[21]

However, this only works as long as you are honest about your monitoring. If you are lying about it, you're only hurting yourself. Our self-protecting mental mechanisms often try to interfere with this, but we can prevent that from happening by focusing on the facts and keeping our emotions and thoughts out of the situation. Focus on your actions and ignore the rest. You either did it or you didn't; it's a yes or a no. It's important to keep this distinction of action being different than emotions because a behavior is only about what we did, not the thoughts that made us do it.

It helps to synchronize your expectations and your behavior by looking at what you are doing, what others expect you to do, and what you expect of yourself. If these three things are not overlapping, you could be stressed. Now, I'm not talking about unrealistic expectations set upon you by others. When I say what others expect you to do, these are things you agreed to, like your boss wanting a project done on a certain date or your roommate expecting you to bring home dish soap.

So let's say you agreed to bring home the dish soap to your roommate, spouse, or friend. However, you completely forgot and get home without the dish soap. Your behavior and expectations were not synchronized, so there are two options here. You can either go back to the store and get dish soap to synchronize the three parts, or you can lower yours and others' expectations by apologizing and saying you'll do it tomorrow. The action expectation then gets postponed until tomorrow so that there isn't any tension caused by the inconsistency between the three parts.

Obviously, the second option isn't the best one. And oftentimes, the situation isn't as black and white as bringing home dish soap. If you're in the middle of your work project and suddenly realize you won't get it done on time, you can't exactly tell your boss, "Sorry, I'll just do it tomorrow." So, what can you do in these types of situations?

When more severe inconsistencies happen in your life, stop for a moment to analyze what's going on. Are you taking on too much work? Or did you get unproductive and procrastinate? There are other questions you can also ask, but find the answers and see what you can improve on now and what you can improve on in the future.

Make three different lists. One is what you are currently doing, the second is what you think others

Two Key Activities for Lasting Change

want you to do, and the third is what you think you should do. Compare these lists and try to understand where the conflict comes from. In the future, make sure you are only saying yes to things that you know you can fulfill.

Finally, clear your head and try to answer the following questions:

- What behavior do I want to change from?
- What behaviors do I want to adopt?
- How will I benefit from this change?
- How will I make these changes work?

With all of these questions, you need to track your progress and monitor yourself. Monitor and track both the short-term and long-term outcomes.

When you're putting effort into monitoring yourself and keeping your motivations high, you'll see that change is actually an exciting thing that you're going to be successful at. Accepting that there are failures along the way and learning from your mistakes is one of the most important things you can do to see lasting change.

Key Takeaways:

- Motivation is important to keep you going, but you don't want to push yourself too hard.
- Keep a journal of everything you accomplish each day and don't do the same things over and over.
- Find the best arousal rate to get your stuff done, and set realistic deadlines that don't give you too much time.
- Monitor your progress and check in with your body to make sure you aren't under too much stress.
- Monitoring yourself actually increases the chance of you making a change last.

10

New Habits for a New Life

Making a change can rely a lot on our habits. When we create a habit, we transfer what is called the action initiation from our conscious to our external cuing mechanisms that work with impulse processing. This helps because our behavior becomes a habit, which then frees up our cognitive resources for other demanding tasks. When we are trying to make a change, a lot of our energy and cognitive capabilities are relied upon. Habits take that away, and it can help make the change a lasting one.

Many studies have shown that creating habits with behavioral change interventions can increase the likelihood of the new behavior sticking. Habits are hard to break, which is why it is so successful in helping with behavioral change. But let's say you have a habit that you want to change. How can you change it?[22]

Evolve Your Habits

How to Change a Habit

Changing a habit isn't as easy as pie, but it can be as easy as one, two, three. Let me introduce you to the three Rs of changing a habit. They are reminder, routine, and reward.

A reminder is a trigger that initiates the habit. Routine is the behavior and action that you are taking. A reward is a benefit you get from doing the behavior. Every habit follows this three-step process, and behavioral psychologists have proven this time and time again.

Charles Duhigg in his book *The Power of Habit* refers to the three steps of what he called the "Habit Loop" as cue, routine, and reward.[23] B.J. Fogg, a well-known Stanford professor, also talks about these three steps, but he uses the word "trigger" instead of cue. However, the three Rs are easy to remember, so that's why I choose to go with reminder.

So, for an example of how the three Rs work, let's break them down with a simple habit of reading a text message.

- Your phone or smartwatch pings, which acts as the reminder that triggers the habit of looking at this text message.
- You open your phone and read the text message, which is the actual routine and behavior happening.
- You find out who texted you and what they said, which serves as the reward of opening your phone and reading the text.

Step by Step Change

Step One

The first step to changing or creating a new habit is to set a reminder. Sure, you want to be motivated enough to remember, but that doesn't always happen. We can't rely on motivation, so we need to set a simple reminder. It can help cement the behavior and stop the excuses in their tracks.

For example, let's say that you want to start exercising in the morning before work. When you're all snuggled up in bed, this is a hard habit to form. However, setting your running shoes right next to your bed and putting your alarm next to the shoes can remind you that you need to go and exercise. You already have the habit of reaching over to your alarm clock and turning it off, but now you'll be linking your new habit of exercise with your old habit of turning off the alarm by setting your shoes right next to it.

This reminder is going to make it easier to start your new habit, but it can be difficult to try and decide what reminder to use. It's obviously going to differ for each person, but writing two lists can help you to choose what reminder works best. The first list should be things that you do every single day without fail.

For example:

- Brush your teeth
- Eat a meal
- Take a shower
- Go to the bathroom
- Lock the door
- Turn off the lights

These are daily habits to you, and you can link a new habit to an already existing habit. It could be something like every time I go to the bathroom, I do five squats.

The next list is going to be things that happen to you every day without fail. This one might be a bit harder to come up with, but let me give you a few examples.

For example:

- You get tagged in a comment on Facebook.
- A commercial interrupts your TV show.
- Someone texts you.

With these two lists, you can easily put together a new habit with something that already happens to you, or something you already do.

For example, you want to drink more water. You could say that every time you eat a meal, you'll drink one glass of water. Even though it's just a glass of water, it could be the start to get you to drink the 12 glasses of water you want to drink each day.

Step Two

The second step is to choose a habit that's easy enough to start. When it's so easy that you can't say no, this is good. Your life goals are not going to be your habits, but your habits can help your life goals.

We all want to make massive changes in our lives, and there's nothing wrong with that. However, it does get a bit overwhelming when we try to tackle it all at once. We want everything right now, and we never want to wait for it. Once we see someone else has lost 100 pounds on TV, we want to lose 100 pounds. But we want to do it by tomorrow. It'd be great if that could happen, but it won't.

We get enthusiastic about making changes in our life, and that's a good thing, but we have to remember that lasting change comes from small habits that add up over time. Start small, and make your habit extremely easy.

B.J. Fogg suggested that you make these habits micro-sized. If you want to increase flossing, just floss one tooth. Yes, that sounds crazy, and you'll probably end up flossing more than one tooth, but who could honestly say no to flossing just one tooth? It probably takes about two seconds.

Your performance doesn't matter when you're first starting out in a new habit. The goal here is to get the behavior to become consistent so that it becomes a habit. First, you have to decide what it is that you want to change. Then ask yourself how you can make it easy enough that you won't be able to refuse it.

What's the Reward?

This is the fun part, because you get to celebrate! Everyone loves to celebrate. Even if you're not the type to throw huge parties and jump for joy, it's still nice to reward yourself. When we feel good, we want to keep doing that thing. And because we keep doing that thing to make ourselves feel good, it becomes a habit.

Your reward can be as simple as getting a treat (as long as your goal isn't to be healthy, lose weight, etc.), or you can do something like just telling yourself that you did a good job. Whatever it is, give yourself some credit for what you have done. Just make it an easy enough reward that it can be repeated each time you do the new behavior.

Some people swear by telling themselves that they did a good job. This is a nice and easy reward that you can start off with. Once you do the habit, tell yourself you're proud of your behavior.

These three steps are going to help you to form your habit, but it's not always as easy as it sounds. It's probably going to take a little bit of experimentation. The first reminder that you choose might not be a winner, so you might have to go through multiple reminders until you find one that fits within your schedule and works with what you do.

Figuring out how to make your habit easy might be difficult too. Sometimes your new habit is a bit more complex than learning to floss or drinking more water.

When that happens, you still have to think about how you can make it easy enough to do every day. It might take a bit, but once you get it down, you'll see a huge difference in how your behavior changes.

And finally, your reward system might take a while too. Telling yourself you've done a good job might not be enough for you, but getting yourself a sweet treat might be too much for you. Maybe you reward yourself with a dollar each time, and once you hit a certain amount, you treat yourself to a massage or trinket you've been wanting. Whatever reward you choose; try to stick with it for at least a few weeks. If it doesn't seem to be working out, switch it.

Key Takeaways:

- Creating a new habit will help you make lasting change and support the goals you set.
- Habits are small daily actions, and they work best when they are attached to an already formed habit.
- Reminder, routine, and reward are the three Rs that are present in habit change.
- It might take some experimentation to get the three Rs to work for you and help you to create a new habit.
- Every habit follows these three steps, no matter how simple or complicated it is.

Conclusion

Change is something we all seem to run away from, but it doesn't have to be like that. While change can seem scary or daunting at first, when made using the advice from this book, it doesn't need to be. Taking that leap can be the best and most exciting thing you have ever done. I've been there!

Saying goodbye to an old behavior that no longer serves you is a good thing, and you'll be leaving behind a dust-ridden life to a life of more joy, contentment, and peace of mind. Change can help you see who you were meant to be, and it's never too late to make it happen. No matter who you are, how old you are, or what your circumstances are like, you can make a positive change and leave behind worry, fear, isolation, and a mediocre life.

If you've wanted to change but have been too scared, just use the tips in this book to get where you want to be. Gather the courage to drop the insecurities and low self-esteem that have been holding you back from living your

Conclusion

best life. Sometimes we choose to change, and sometimes we are forced to change because of our circumstances; the best strategy you can have for both of them is to prepare your mind to deal with both when the time comes. You can learn to expect the unexpected and create a better life.

I want to thank you all for spending the time to read this book. It's been a fun, crazy, and exciting journey studying, writing, and putting all I've learned from my own experiences into words for others to read. I sincerely hope that you will take the advice written here to better your own lives, and I wish you all the success in doing so.

Now, take what you've learned and show the world just how badass you are! If you've enjoyed reading this book and feel it could help someone you know, please share it with them. The more we all know, the better we all are.

I wish you the best of luck!

Yours,

Zoe

References

American Psychological Association. *Willpower. Introduction.* American Psychological Association. 2018. http://www.apa.org/helpcenter/willpower.aspx

Anholt, Robert R.H. and Trudy F.C. Mackay. *Principles of Behavioral Genetics.* Academic Press. ISBN 978-0-12-372575-2. Lay summary. 2010.

Brenner, Abigail. *How to Change Your Good Behavior?* Psychology Today. 2013. https://www.psychologytoday.com/blog/influx/201306/how-change-your-behavior-good

Console India Inc. *Understanding Human Behavior.* Console India Inc. 2014. http://www.consoleindiainc.com/2014/09/11/understanding-human-behavior/

Duhigg, Charles. *The Power of Habit.* Random House Trade Paperbacks. 2014.

Dweck, Carol S. *Mindset: The New Psychology of Success.* Ballantine Books. 2007.

Fogg, B.J. *Tiny Habits.* 2018. http://tinyhabits.com

Fremouw, William J. and John P. Brown, Jr. *The Reactivity of Addictive Behaviors to Self-Monitoring: A Functional Analysis.* West Virginia University, Morgantown, WV, USA. 2002. https://doi.org/10.1016/0306-4603(80)90041-6

Gardner, Benjamin. *Habit Formation and Behavior Change.* Oxford Research Encyclopedias. Psychology. 2018. http://psychology.oxfordre.com/view/10.1093/acrefore/9780190236557.001.0001/acrefore-9780190236557-e-129

Health Promotion Unit, 2007. *Stages of Behavior Change: Queensland Stay On Your Feet® Community Good Practice Toolkit.* Division of Chief Health Officer, Queensland Health. 2018. https://www.health.qld.gov.au/__data/assets/pdf_file/0026/425960/33331.pdf

Kendra, Cherry. *What Is Classical Conditioning? A Step-by-Step Guide to How Classical Conditioning Really Works.* Very Well. 2017. https://www.verywell.com/classical-conditioning-2794859

Kendra, Cherry. *What Is Maslow's Hierarchy of Needs?* Very Well. 2018. https://www.verywell.com/what-is-maslows-hierarchy-of-needs-4136760

Kendra, Cherry. *What Is the Yerkes-Dodson law and performance?* Very Well. 2017. https://www.verywell.com/what-is-the-yerkes-dodson-law-2796027

Learning Theories. *Classical and Operant Conditioning.* Learning Theories. 2018. https://www.learning-theories.com/operant-conditioning-skinner.html

Lieberman, Matthew D. *Social Cognitive Neuroscience: A Review of Core Processes.* Annual Review of Psychology 58:259–89. 2007. http://www.scn.ucla.edu/pdf/Lieberman%20(2006)%20Ann%20Review.pdf

Mind Tools Team. *SMART Goals: How to Make Your Goals Achievable?* Mind Tools. 2018. https://www.mindtools.com/pages/article/smart-goals.htm

Prochaska, J.O. and W.F. Velicer. *The Transtheoretical Model of Health Behavior Change.* American Journal of Health Promotion AJHP 12(1):38–48. 1997.

References

Psychology Today. *Cognitive Dissonance.* Psychology Today. 2018. https://www.psychologytoday.com/us/basics/cognitive-dissonance

Spilka, B. and D.N. McIntosh. *The Psychology of Religion.* Westview Press. 1996.

Tanggaard, L. *The Sociomateriality of Creativity in Everyday Life.* 20–21. Sage Journals. 2013. http://cap.sagepub.com/content/19/1/20.full.pdf+html

Tangney, J.P., J. Stuewig, and D.J. Mashek. *Moral Emotions and Moral Behavior.* Annual Review of Psychology, 58: 345. 2007.

The Best Brain Possible. *The Neuroscience of Changing Your Behavior.* The Best Brain Possible. 2017. https://www.thebestbrainpossible.com/the-neuroscience-of-changing-your-behavior/

Your Dictionary. *Operant Conditioning Examples.* Your Dictionary. 2018. http://examples.yourdictionary.com/operant-conditioning-examples.html

Endnotes

1. Console India Inc. *Understanding Human Behavior*. Console India Inc. 2014. http://www.consoleindiainc.com/2014/09/11/understanding-human-behavior/
2. Anholt, Robert R.H. and Trudy F.C. Mackay. *Principles of Behavioral Genetics*. Academic Press. ISBN 978-0-12-372575-2. Lay summary. 2010.
3. Tanggaard, L. *The Sociomateriality of Creativity in Everyday Life*. 20–21. Sage Journals. 2013. http://cap.sagepub.com/content/19/1/20.full.pdf+html
4. Spilka, B. and D.N. McIntosh *The Psychology of Religion*. Westview Press. 1996.
5. Tangney, J.P., J. Stuewig, and D.J. Mashek. *Moral Emotions and Moral Behavior*. Annual Review of Psychology, 58: 345. 2007.
6. Lieberman, Matthew D. *Social Cognitive Neuroscience: A Review of Core Processes*. Annual Review of Psychology 58:259–89. 2007. http://www.scn.ucla.edu/pdf/Lieberman%20(2006)%20Ann%20Review.pdf
7. The Best Brain Possible. *The Neuroscience of Changing Your Behavior*. The Best Brain Possible. 2017. https://www.thebestbrainpossible.com/the-neuroscience-of-changing-your-behavior/

8 Cherry, Kendra. *What Is Classical Conditioning? A Step-by-Step Guide to How Classical Conditioning Really Works.* Very Well. 2017. https://www.verywell.com/classical-conditioning-2794859

9 Learning Theories. *Classical and Operant Conditioning.* Learning Theories. 2018. https://www.learning-theories.com/operant-conditioning-skinner.html

10 Your Dictionary. *Operant Conditioning Examples.* Your Dictionary. 2018. http://examples.yourdictionary.com/operant-conditioning-examples.html

11 Fogg, B.J. *Tiny Habits.* 2018. http://tinyhabits.com

12 Health Promotion Unit, 2007. *Stages of Behavior Change: Queensland Stay On Your Feet® Community Good Practice Toolkit.* Division of Chief Health Officer, Queensland Health. 2018. https://www.health.qld.gov.au/__data/assets/pdf_file/0026/425960/33331.pdf

13 Prochaska, J.O. and W.F. Velicer. *The Transtheoretical Model of Health Behavior Change.* American Journal of Health Promotion AJHP 12(1):38–48. 1997.

14 Dweck, Carol S. *Mindset: The New Psychology of Success.* Ballantine Books. 2007.

15 American Psychological Association. *Willpower. Introduction.* American Psychological Association. 2018. http://www.apa.org/helpcenter/willpower.aspx

16 Psychology Today. *Cognitive Dissonance.* Psychology Today. 2018. https://www.psychologytoday.com/us/basics/cognitive-dissonance

17 Kendra, Cherry. *What Is Maslow's Hierarchy of Needs?* Very Well. 2018. https://www.verywell.com/what-is-maslows-hierarchy-of-needs-4136760

18 Brenner, Abigail. *How to Change Your Good Behavior?* Psychology Today. 2013. https://www.psychologytoday.com/blog/in-flux/201306/how-change-your-behavior-good

19 Mind Tools Team. *SMART Goals: How to Make Your Goals Achievable?* Mind Tools. 2018. https://www.mindtools.com/pages/article/smart-goals.htm

20 Kendra, Cherry. *What Is the Yerkes-Dodson law and performance?* Very Well. 2017. https://www.verywell.com/what-is-the-yerkes-dodson-law-2796027

21 Fremouw, William J. and John P. Brown, Jr. *The Reactivity of Addictive Behaviors to Self-Monitoring: A Functional Analysis.* West Virginia University, Morgantown, WV, USA. 2002. https://doi.org/10.1016/0306-4603(80)90041-6

22 Gardner, Benjamin. *Habit Formation and Behavior Change.* Oxford Research Encyclopedias. Psychology. 2018. http://psychology.oxfordre.com/view/10.1093/acrefore/9780190236557.001.0001/acrefore-9780190236557-e-129

23 Duhigg, Charles. *The Power of Habit.* Random House Trade Paperbacks. 2014.